ARACHNID WORLD
BLACK WIDOWS

SANDRA MARKLE

LERNER PUBLICATIONS COMPANY MINNEAPOLIS

FOR CURIOUS KIDS EVERYWHERE

ACKNOWLEDGMENTS

The author would like to thank, Dr. Nadia Ayoub, University of California, Riverside; Dr. Todd Blackledge, University of Akron; Dr. Jessica Garb, University of Massachusetts, Lowell; and Dr. Simon Pollard, Canterbury Museum, Christchurch, New Zealand, for sharing their expertise and enthusiasm. A special thanks to Skip Jeffery for his support during the creation of this book.

Lerner Publications Company
A division of Lerner Publishing Group, Inc.
241 First Avenue North
Minneapolis, MN 55401 U.S.A.

Website address: www.lernerbooks.com

Library of Congress Cataloging-in-Publication Data

Markle, Sandra.
    Black widows : deadly biters / by Sandra Markle.
      p.   cm. — (Arachnid world)
    Includes bibliographical references and index.
    ISBN 978–0–7613–5038–5 (lib. bdg. : alk. paper)
    1. Black widow spider—Juvenile literature. I. Title.
QL458.42.T54M37 2011
595.4′4—dc22   2010004274

Manufactured in the United States of America
1 - PC - 12/31/10

CONTENTS

AN ARACHNID'S WORLD

WELCOME TO THE WORLD OF ARACHNIDS

(ah-RACK-nidz). Arachnids can be found everywhere on Earth except in the deep ocean.

So how can you tell if an animal is an arachnid rather than a relative like the insect shown below? Both arachnids and insects belong to a group of animals called arthropods (AR-throh-podz). All the animals in this group share some traits. They have bodies divided into segments, jointed legs, and a stiff exoskeleton. This is a skeleton on the outside like a suit of armor. But one way to tell if an animal is an arachnid is to count its legs and main body parts. While not every adult arachnid has eight legs, most do. Arachnids also have two main body parts. Adult insects, like this hornet *(above)*, have six legs and three main body parts.

This book is about black widow spiders. Almost all spiders are venomous, meaning they kill prey by injecting a liquid poison. A black widow's venom is very strong. It can kill prey bigger than many other kinds of spiders can tackle.

BLACK WIDOW FACT

A black widow spider's body temperature rises and falls with the temperature around it. It must warm up to be active.

OUTSIDE AND INSIDE

ON THE OUTSIDE

There are about thirty different types of black widow spiders. They all share certain features. They all have two main body parts: the cephalothorax (sef-uh-loh-THOR-ax) and the abdomen. A waistlike part called the pedicel joins the two. The spider's exoskeleton is made up of many plates. Stretchy tissues connect the plates so the spider can bend and move.

Take a close look at the outside of a female black widow spider to discover other key features.

LEGS:
These are used for walking and building webs.

CLAWS:
These are at the tips of the legs and help the spider grip its silk threads.

CHELICERAE (keh-LISS-ee-ray): This pair of jawlike parts is near the mouth and ends in fangs. The fangs are used to stab prey and inject venom.

PEDIPALPS: These are a pair of leglike parts that extend from the head near the mouth. They help catch prey and hold it for eating. In males the pedipalps are also used during reproduction.

CEPHALOTHORAX

PEDICEL

ABDOMEN

ON THE INSIDE

Look inside an adult female black widow spider.

HEART: This muscular tube pumps blood throughout the body cavity and organs.

VENOM GLAND: This body part produces venom.

BRAIN: The part that sends and receives messages to and from body parts.

PHARYNX (FAR-inks): This muscular tube pumps food into the stomach. Hairs in the tube help filter out solid waste.

NERVE GANGLIA: These bundles of nerve tissue send messages between the brain and other body parts.

COXAL (KAHK-sehl) GLANDS: These special groups of cells collect liquid wastes and pass them through openings to the outside.

SUCKING STOMACH: The stomach works with the pharynx to move food between the mouth and the intestines. Cells in the lining produce digestive juices.

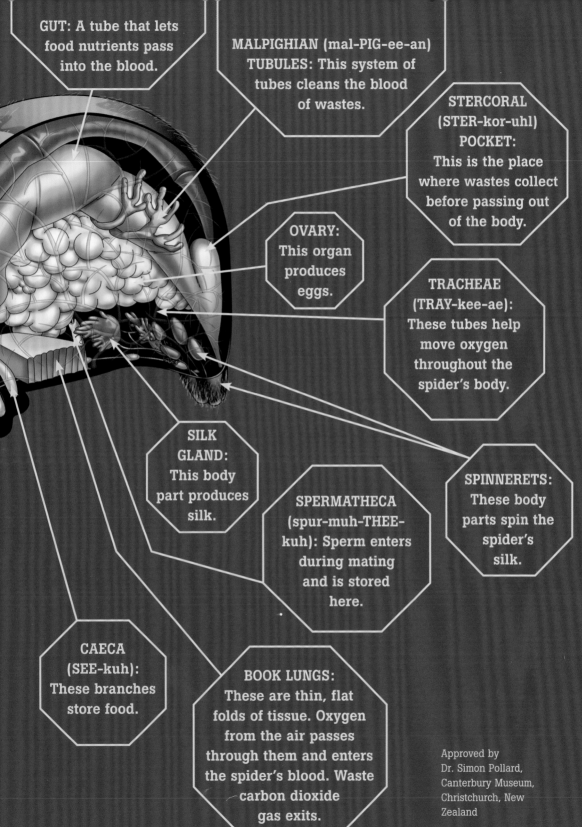

GUT: A tube that lets food nutrients pass into the blood.

MALPIGHIAN (mal-PIG-ee-an) TUBULES: This system of tubes cleans the blood of wastes.

STERCORAL (STER-kor-uhl) POCKET: This is the place where wastes collect before passing out of the body.

OVARY: This organ produces eggs.

TRACHEAE (TRAY-kee-ae): These tubes help move oxygen throughout the spider's body.

SILK GLAND: This body part produces silk.

SPERMATHECA (spur-muh-THEE-kuh): Sperm enters during mating and is stored here.

SPINNERETS: These body parts spin the spider's silk.

CAECA (SEE-kuh): These branches store food.

BOOK LUNGS: These are thin, flat folds of tissue. Oxygen from the air passes through them and enters the spider's blood. Waste carbon dioxide gas exits.

Approved by Dr. Simon Pollard, Canterbury Museum, Christchurch, New Zealand

BECOMING ADULTS

Like all arachnids, black widows go through incomplete metamorphosis. *Metamorphosis* means "change." A black widow spider's life includes three stages: egg, nymph or spiderling, and adult.

Spiderlings hatch from their eggs blind and unable to eat. They stay in the protection of the egg sac their mother spun to hold her eggs. After a few days, they molt, or shed their skin. Then they can see and begin to eat. Their first meal may be a weaker brother or sister. They also begin to chew on the wall of the egg sac. As they chew, their digestive juices help break down the sac walls. When a hole opens in it, the spiderlings crawl out. They head off to live on their own.

Compare these southern black widow spiderlings to the adult. They are smaller. Their coloring and markings are also a little different. Even so, they can do anything adults can do except mate and produce young.

> **SOME KINDS OF ARTHROPODS GO THROUGH COMPLETE METAMORPHOSIS.** The four stages are egg, larva, pupa, and adult. Each stage looks and behaves very differently.

BLACK WIDOW FACT

Four kinds of black widows are native to the United States. They are the western black widows, the eastern black widows, the southern black widows, and the red widows.

EGG

SPIDERLINGS

ADULT

STRONG SILK AND VENOM

The black widow spider spends its life hunting. It catches its prey in a web made of silk. The black widow produces many different kinds of silk from its spinnerets. One kind of silk, dragline silk, is among the strongest natural fibers in the world. The spider uses its strong silk to build a web trap. After prey is trapped, the spider wraps it up in sticky silk *(below)* to anchor it in the web.

To kill its prey, a black widow produces strong venom. This venom is a neurotoxin. That means it acts on the prey's nervous system and paralyzes it, so it can't move. This way, a black widow spider can kill prey, such as this scorpion *(below)*, that is too big and strong for many other kinds of spiders.

BLACK WIDOW FACT

Black widows usually only bite people if they are squeezed or bumped by them.

SPIDERLINGS AWAY!

It's a warm summer day when a female western black widow spiderling leaves her egg sac. She is hungry and ready for a meal. First, though, she needs to get away from her hungry brothers and sisters *(right)*. She climbs out onto her mother's web and pulls a strand of dragline silk out of her spinnerets. The wind catches her silk strand and blows her away. The spiderling travels wherever the wind takes her.

When the breeze slows down, the spiderling drops and lands. She doesn't find any shelter, so she keeps traveling. Soon she stops again and pulls out another dragline. This time she also rubs her rear end on the ground. At the same time, she produces another kind of silk. This silk cements the dragline to the ground. Then the spiderling moves on, letting out more silk. Her silk strand becomes a safety line. When she drops off a rock, it's like falling off a cliff to her. But like a bungee jumper, she only drops as far as the anchored line reaches. She can continue downward by spinning more silk or climbing back up her line.

BLACK WIDOW FACT

Silk starts as a gooey liquid shot through special nozzles in the spider's spinnerets. The liquid becomes a solid strand when the spider fastens it to something—even its own leg—and pulls.

SPINNERETS

SPINNING TO EAT

The black widow spiderling doesn't go far before she finds a sheltered crack close to the ground. This will be her home. She starts to spin silk again. This time, she's building a web to hide her home. She's also building a snare to trap prey. She starts with a few strands of dragline silk. They spread from her home like the spokes from the hub of a bicycle wheel. Below this, she loops lots of crisscrossing silk threads to form a tangled sheet called a cobweb. Finally, she spins glue-coated traplines. These are also called sticky gum-footed lines.

To construct each trapline, the spider first drops straight down from her web to the ground pulling out a silk strand.

BLACK WIDOW FACT

The webs of a black widow spider have no regular shape.

STICKY GUM-FOOTED TRAPLINE

She anchors this to the ground with a little dab of silk glue. Next, she starts to climb back up the strand, spinning a second silk thread. This one is coated with glue droplets. The spider climbs about 1 inch (2.5 centimeters) up the first strand. At that point, she bites through the glue-coated thread and lightly glues the two lines together. Then she climbs up the rest of the original line to her web. She spins nearly twenty more traplines this same way. Then she settles into her home with her feet touching her web's main lines.

When an ant walks into one of her traplines, the spider can feel it. Snap! The silk line breaks and yanks the ant off its feet. The young female black widow pulls up her first meal.

Like all black widows, the female western black widow spends her life focused on hunting. She has eight big eyes, but she doesn't see clearly. So she doesn't go searching for prey. Instead, she hides in plain sight by sitting still. She looks like a shadow on her web. She might also hide nearby, holding onto her web strands with her feet. Once settled, she waits for prey to come to her trap.

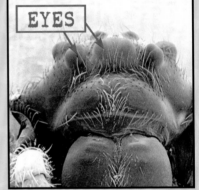

EYES

If she senses that whatever is moving her web is too large and strong, she leaves it alone. If she senses the animal is prey-sized, like this insect *(facing page)*, she charges. Hairs on the black widow's legs and feet alert her to movement in her web. Claws help her grip her web threads as she runs across the strands.

HAIRY FOOT

When she gets close to the prey, she throws sticky silk over it. This stops the prey from struggling. Then she bites whatever part she can safely reach, such as a leg. Her fangs poke through the insect's exoskeleton. A few drops of venom pour out of a tiny hole near each fang tip.

In addition to claws, black widows have rows of strong bristles on their hind pair of legs. They use these comblike bristles to toss silk over prey, helping to trap it.

In humans a black widow's bite causes muscle pain, stomach cramps, nausea, and difficulty breathing. It can be fatal. But people can be treated with antivenin, a chemical that counteracts the venom.

The female pulls back after she bites. Most likely, she injected some digestive juices with her venom. But to be sure, once the prey is quiet, she bites again. This time, she injects more digestive juices. Then she waits again. The digestive juices turn the prey's soft tissue into a kind of liquid power drink. The muscles around the spider's pharynx and stomach relax, creating a sucking force. This force pulls the liquid food out of the prey's exoskeleton and into the spider's body. Then the spider injects more digestive juices and repeats the process.

Finally, only the prey's empty exoskeleton remains. The black widow cuts this garbage loose and lets it drop out of her web. If a section of the web is damaged, she repairs it.

GROWING APPETITE

The young black widow eats and grows bigger. Before long, she is too big for her exoskeleton. It is time to molt, so she spins a special silk thread. As she hangs upside down from this thread, her exoskeleton splits open. When the young spider crawls out of the old skin, she is already covered by a new exoskeleton. This new covering is soft. Her heart pumps, forcing blood throughout her body to stretch her soft exoskeleton. The stretched exoskeleton will give her room to grow before she has to molt again. While she waits for her new coat to harden, she hides from predators. She doesn't attack prey.

BLACK WIDOW FACT

With each molt, the immature western black widow becomes blacker. This is true of most kinds of black widows. She also develops belly markings and loses the markings on her back.

EMPTY EXOSKELETON

SPIDER STRETCHING
NEW EXOSKELETON

As the young female black widow grows bigger, she expands her web to catch bigger prey. But she's also become big enough so that predators, such as wasps and birds, can spot her more easily. The young spider spins more silk to thicken one part of her web. During the day, she hides in this protected space *(opposite page)*. She only rushes out onto her web to attack trapped prey. Once her venom has done its job, she will often cut loose her prey. Then she grips the takeaway meal in her chelicerae and carries it to her safe space before eating it.

BLACK WIDOW FACT

Not all female black widows have a red hourglass shape on their abdomen. But like this Mediterranean black widow *(below)*, all have some kind of bright markings. These warn predators: LEAVE ME ALONE!

THE CYCLE CONTINUES

It is late summer, and some leaves are already turning gold and red. Grasshoppers and crickets and other prey insects have grown into mature adults. So has the female western black widow spider. She's reached her full adult size. She's about 0.5 inches (1.3 cm) long and weighs about 0.04 ounces (1 gram). She's big enough to catch even larger prey, such as this cricket *(right)*. Eating large prey gives her an energy boost. It's what she needs to produce eggs.

Ready to mate, the adult female replaces some of the silk strands of her web. She produces chemicals called pheromones (FEHR-uh-mohnz) to coat these strands.

BLACK WIDOW FACT

As long as a spiderling is growing and molting, it may be able to regrow a lost body part, such as a leg. The new part develops, folded up inside the exoskeleton at the injury site. It unfolds during the next molt.

A mature male western black widow spider detects the female's pheromones like perfume in the air. He gets ready to mate by spinning a tiny web. On this, he deposits a small amount of sperm, or male reproductive cells. Then he picks up the web with his paddle-shaped pedipalps. He tracks the western black widow female's pheromones to find her.

Like all black widow spider couples, the male is less than half the size of the female. She could easily overpower him. And she doesn't see well enough to recognize him as a mating male. So before he enters her web, he plucks her web threads. This signals his intentions. The female black widow doesn't move as he comes closer.

BLACK WIDOW FACT

Each kind of black widow spider produces its own pheromones. A western black widow female only attracts a western black widow male.

MALE

FEMALE

Finally, the male is close enough to touch the female. He spins web threads around her. She could easily break free, but she still doesn't move.

An adult female is about as big as a paper clip. A male is no bigger than a grain of rice.

The male inserts his sperm cells into the female's gonopore (reproductive opening). Then he quickly exits the female's web.

Searching for a female and mating takes a lot of energy. The male may die shortly afterward. Or he may live long enough to search out another female and mate again before dying.

BLACK WIDOW FACT

Most kinds of female black widow spiders do not eat their mates. But one kind of Australian black widow often does.

Alone again, the female black widow breaks free of the male's web. A short time later, she starts spinning. She is creating a small web as a base for her eggs. Onto this, one at a time, she deposits a cluster of more than one hundred eggs. As each egg leaves her body, it passes by the stored sperm. When a sperm joins with an egg cell, the egg develops a tough coating. Inside, a baby spider starts to grow.

Next, the female western black widow spins a sturdy silk egg sac in which to wrap the egg cluster. The sac will protect her eggs from rain, cold, and drying out in the heat of the sun. She guards the egg sac from predators. A few kinds of female wasps and flies try to insert their own eggs into the spider's egg sac. If they succeed, the young wasp or fly grows up feeding on the black widow's eggs.

BLACK WIDOW FACT

Many female black widows divide their eggs among several egg sacs. Then if anything happens to one sac, the eggs in the other sacs stay safe.

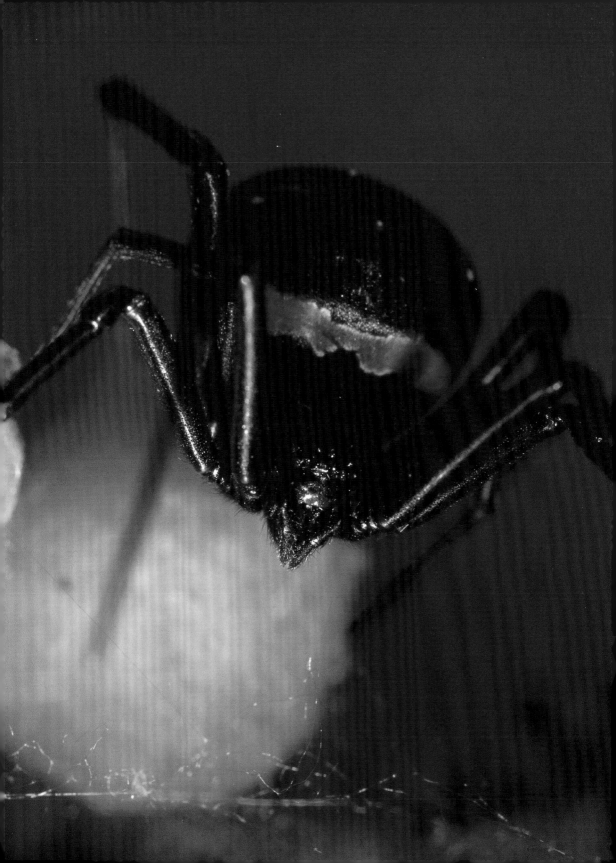

Inside their eggs in the egg sac, the baby spiders grow for about three to four weeks. Meanwhile, the female stays alert for movements on her web threads. She attacks any intruders and eats whatever she catches. This keeps her eggs safe. It also gives her the energy she needs to stay on guard duty.

EGGS INSIDE AN EGG SAC

The baby spiders develop until they nearly fill their eggs. Then they use hard bumps near their mouths, called egg teeth, to break them open. The blind newly hatched spiderlings stay put in the egg sac for a few more days until they molt for the first time. Then they start chewing on the egg sac wall. They give off digestive juices that help break down the egg sac. The spiderlings finally break through and leave the sac.

ONE-DAY-OLD BABY SPIDERS INSIDE EGG SAC

Some black widow spiders, like these northern black widows, live where winters are cold. There, the babies don't develop and hatch until the weather warms up again. But whenever they come out, their mother is probably still on guard duty. She doesn't provide any care for the spiderlings. But she does attack any intruders. This means that until the spiderlings leave the web, she keeps her babies safe just by being there.

BLACK WIDOW FACT

Where winters are cold, black widows may move indoors before laying their eggs. To help keep black widows outside, be sure screens fit snugly. Also seal doors with weather stripping.

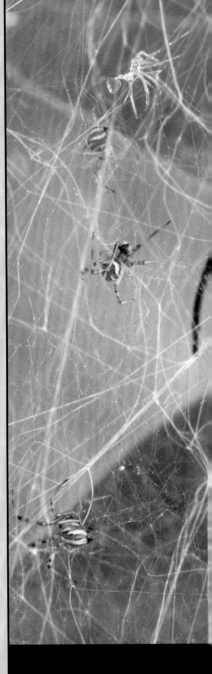

Mature female black widows may live for several years. But only a few black widow spiderlings live long enough to grow up. Most become prey for other predators. Those that survive depend on their powerful venom to catch prey. This way they get the energy they need to grow bigger and to mature. One day, they'll also mate and produce young. Generation after generation, the cycle of black widows and their hunting life continues.

BLACK WIDOWS AND OTHER VENOMOUS ARACHNIDS

BLACK WIDOW SPIDERS belong to a group, or order, of arachnids called Aranea (ah-RAHN-ee-ay). This order contains the spider members of the arachnid group. Black widow spiders belong to a family of spiders, the Theridiidae (thehr-uh-DY-eh-dee). The spiders in this family build messy-looking webs, called cobwebs. Black widows also belong to a particular group within this family, the *Latrodectus* (la-troh-DEK-tuhs) spiders. *Latrodectus* spiders produce strong venom that attacks the nervous system.

SCIENTISTS GROUP living and extinct animals with others that are similar. So black widow spiders are classified this way:

> kingdom: Animalia
> phylum: Arthropoda
> class: Arachnida
> order: Araneae
> family: Theridiidae
> genus: *Latrodectus*

HELPFUL OR HARMFUL? Black widow spiders are both. They're helpful because they eat a lot of insects. This helps control the numbers of insects that could otherwise become pests. They're harmful because, while they only bite in self-defense, their venom is strong enough to make people ill. Rarely, their bite may even kill.

HOW BIG IS a western black widow spider? A female is about 1.25 inches (3 cm) long, including the legs.

MORE VENOMOUS ARACHNIDS

Black widows don't have the strongest venom of any spider. But they are one of the best-known spiders with strong venom. That's because they live in lots of different parts of the world. Compare the venom of these other venomous arachnids to the venom produced by black widows.

Brazilian Wandering Spiders are listed in *Guinness World Records* as the world's most venomous spider. Their venom causes paralysis and breathing difficulties that can be fatal. An antivenin is available. These spiders are large, with a leg span up to 5 inches (12.7 cm). The Brazilian wandering spiders are found in tropical Central and South America. They do not build a web as a retreat or a trap. Instead, they wander the forest floor in search of prey, such as insects, lizards, and mice.

Fat-tailed Scorpions live in the deserts of the Middle East and Africa. They are considered among the most venomous scorpions in the world. Their very strong venom is injected by their stinger tails and is deadly to people. The venom is also being used to treat a type of brain cancer. Fat-tailed scorpions are large (about 5 inches, or 12 cm long). They hide during the day and hunt at night, usually catching their prey with their pincerlike pedipalps. Their venomous sting is mainly for self-defense.

Pseudoscorpions look like scorpions without tails. They inject their venom with a pinch of their claws. Pseudoscorpions are tiny predators (only about 0.5 inch, or 1 cm long). They can be found worldwide. They hunt little insects and spiders. Like spiders, pseudoscorpions produce silk. But instead of producing it from spinnerets, they spin silk from their chelicerae (the jawlike mouthparts). They don't spin webs. But they do use their silk to help them catch their prey.

GLOSSARY

abdomen: the rear end of an arachnid. It contains systems for digestion, reproduction, and, in spiders, silk production.

adult: the reproductive stage of an arachnid's life cycle

book lungs: thin, flat folds of tissue where blood circulates. Air passes through them, allowing oxygen to enter the spider's blood. Waste carbon dioxide gas is given off through them.

brain: the organ that receives messages from the rest of the body and sends signals to control all body parts

caeca: branching tubes through which liquid food passes and where food is stored. Food nutrients pass from the tubes into the blood and are carried throughout the body.

cephalothorax: the front end of an arachnid. It includes the mouth, the brain, and the eyes, if there are any. Legs are also attached to this part.

chelicerae: a pair of jawlike parts that extend from the head in front of the mouth and that end in fangs. The fangs are used to stab prey and inject venom.

coxal glands: a special group of cells for collecting and getting rid of liquid wastes through openings to the outside of the body. They aid in maintaining water balance in the body.

egg: a female reproductive cell; also the name given to the first stage of an arachnid's life cycle

exoskeleton: a protective, armorlike covering on the outside of the body

eyes: sensory organs that detect light and send messages to the brain for sight

fangs: a pair of toothlike parts on the spider's chelicerae. Venom flows out of the fang through a hole near the tip.

heart: the muscular tube that pumps blood throughout the body

Malpighian tubules: a system of tubes that cleans the blood of wastes and dumps them into the intestine

molt: the process of an arachnid shedding its exoskeleton

nerve ganglia: bundles of nerve tissue that send messages between the brain and other body parts

ovary: the body part that produces eggs

pedicel: the waistlike part in spiders that connects the cephalothorax to the abdomen

pedipalps: a pair of leglike body parts that extend from the head near the mouth. Pedipalps help catch prey and hold it for eating. In males the pedipalps are also used to carry the sperm sac.

pharynx: a muscular body part that contracts to create a pumping force, drawing food into the body's digestive system. Hairs filter out hard waste bits.

pheromones: chemicals given off as a form of communication, especially for mating

silk gland: the body part that produces silk

sperm: a male reproductive cell

spermatheca: a sac in female arachnids that stores sperm after mating

spiderling: the name given to the stage between egg and adult in spiders

spinneret: the body part that spins silk

spiracle: a small opening in the exoskeleton that leads into the trachea

stercoral pocket: a place where body wastes collect before passing out through the anus

sucking stomach: the muscular stomach that along with the pharynx pulls liquid food into the arachnid's gut. Cells in the lining produce digestive juices.

tracheae: tubes that help spread oxygen throughout the spider's body. They also store oxygen.

venom: liquid poison

venom gland: the body part that produces venom

DIGGING DEEPER

To keep on investigating black widow spiders, explore these books and on-line sites.

BOOKS

Macro, Chris, Karen Harley, and Philip Taylor. *Black Widow Spider*. Portsmouth, NH: Heinemann, 2003. Take another close-up look at how black widow spiders live and reproduce.

Markle, Sandra. *Sneaky Spinning Baby Spiders*. New York: Walker Books for Young Readers, 2008. Compare how black widow spiderlings hatch and grow up to the life cycles of other kinds of spiders.

Murawski, Darlyne. *Spiders and Their Webs*. Washington, DC: National Geographic Children's Books, 2004. Compare the black widow spider's web spinning to that of other spiderweb builders.

Singer, Marilyn. *Venom*. Minneapolis: Millbrook Press, 2007. Find out about creatures that can harm or even kill with a bite or sting.

Souza, D. M., *Packed with Poison!* Minneapolis: Millbrook Press, 2006. Learn about the most venomous and poisonous animals in the world.

MORE FROM SANDRA MARKLE

INSECT WORLD:
Diving Beetles
Hornets
Locusts
Luna Moths
Mosquitoes
Praying Mantises
Stick Insects
Termites

WEBSITES

Black Widow Spiders

http://sheppardsoftware.com/content/animals/animals/invertebrates/
blackwidowspider.htm

Discover lots of fascinating facts about this spider, and use the site's table of contents to compare it to other arachnids. Then take the spider quiz.

Ten Most Dangerous Spiders in the World

http://www.avivadirectory.com/trivia/42-the-ten-most-dangerous
-spiders-in-the-world

Find out how the black widow spider ranks on this list.

Unraveling the Science behind Black Widow Spider Silk

http://www.scientificamerican.com/podcast/episode.cfm?id=219703AE
-E7F2-99DF-3283A4485F3C12BA

Take a minute to listen to why black widow spider dragline silk is special.

Way of the Warrior:
The Widow Warrior

http://videos.howstuffworks.com/
animal-planet/6752-way-of-the
-warrior-the-widow-warrior-video
.htm

See for yourself how female black widow spiders snare, kill, and eat prey.

LERNER e SOURCE™

Visit www.lerneresource.com **for free, downloadable arachnid diagrams, research assignments to use with this series, and additional information about arachnid scientific names.**

BLACK WIDOW ACTIVITY

A black widow's dragline silk is valued because it's both strong and stretchy. It's only about half as strong as a steel strand of the same thickness, but it's lighter than the steel. And unlike steel, the spider's silk is able to stretch as much as 40 percent of its length without breaking. So how does a human hair compare in strength and stretchiness? Follow these steps to find out.

1. Collect a hair that is at least 6 inches (15 cm) long.

2. Place one end of a popsicle stick across the zero end of a ruler. Position it so it forms an L shape. Tape across the end of the ruler, anchoring the stick.

3. Tape one end of the hair to the end of the popsicle stick. Wrap the tape around the stick.

4. Tape the other end of the hair to a small paper clip. Be sure one part of the clip is free of tape.

5. Bend other paper clips into hooks to form small weights.

6. Have a partner hold the ruler vertically. Hook the bent paper clips, one at a time, onto the clip at the end of the hair. Or if you run out of room, hook them onto one another. Check how much the hair stretches each time another clip is added. How close to 40 percent of its length (about 2.4 inches, or 6 cm) will the hair stretch before it breaks?

INDEX

PHOTO ACKNOWLEDGMENTS

The images in this book are used with the permission of: © Dr. Elmar Billig, p. 4; © Doug Sokell/Visuals Unlimited, Inc., p. 5; © John Cancalosi/National Geographic/Getty Images, pp. 6-7; © Bill Hauser/Independent Picture Service, pp. 8-9; © Robinson, James/Animals Animals, p. 11 (top); © Bockowski, Jim/Animals Animals, p. 11 (bottom); © TC Nature/Animals Animals, p. 12; © OSF/Ramage, A./Animals Animals, p. 13; © Tina Carvalho/Oxford Scientific/Photolibrary, p. 14; © Bryan Reynolds/PHOTOTAKE Inc./Alamy, p. 15; Dr. Todd Blackledge, University of Akron, p. 16; © Joe Warfel/Eighth-Eye Photography, pp. 17, 19; © Jim Zuckerman/CORBIS, p. 18 (top); © Boston Museum of Science/Visuals Unlimited, Inc., p. 18 (bottom); © Bryan E. Reynolds, pp. 20-21, 23, 38-39; © Franceso Tomasinelli/Photo Researchers, Inc., p. 24; © Willis, G.W./Animals Animals, p. 25; © Daniel Heuclin/NHPA/Photoshot, pp. 26-27, 28-29, 30, 31, 41 (middle); © Heidi & Hans-Juergen Koch/Minden Pictures, pp. 32-33; © Dr. Gary D. Gaugler/PHOTOTAKE Inc./Alamy, pp. 34, 35; © Nature's Images/Photo Researchers, Inc., pp. 36-37; © age fotostock/SuperStock, p. 41 (top); © James Carmichael Jr/NHPA/Photoshot, p. 41 (bottom); © Bill Beatty/Visuals Unlimited, Inc., p. 47.

Front cover: © Steve Maslowski/Visuals Unlimited, Inc.